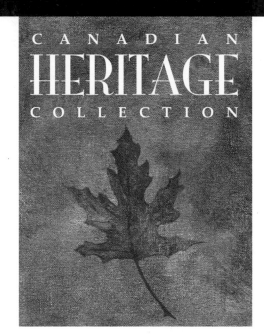

CANADIAN
HERITAGE
COLLECTION

ADVERTISING
REFLECTIONS OF CULTURE AND VALUES

Rose Fine-Meyer & Stephanie K. Gibson

Series Editor
Don Kendal

Ru'bicon

To Carl and Elliot
for their love and support
ROSE FINE-MEYER

To my mother, my father, and my very special
younger sisters who are always close to me,
no matter how great the distance.
STEPHANIE K. GIBSON

Ru'bicon   © 2002 Rubicon Education

ISBN 0-921156-73-1

Editorial Coordinator: Martine Quibell
Production Coordinator: Jennifer Drew
Design: Jennifer Drew

National Library of Canada Cataloguing in Publication
Fine-Meyer, Rose
    Advertising: Reflections of Culture and Values / Rose Fine-Meyer, Stephanie K. Gibson.

(Canadian Heritage Collection)
Includes bibliographical references and index.
ISBN 0-921156-73-1

    1. Advertising–Social aspects–Canada. I. Gibson, Stephanie K.
II. Title. III. Series: Canadian Heritage Collection (Oakville, Ont.)

HF5821.F55 2002   659.1'042'0971   C2002-902018-2

1 2 3 4 5 6 7 8 9 10 – 11 10 09 08 07 06 05 04 03 02

Printed in Canada

COVER:
"To the Canadian Farm," circa 1920
Artist: J. Gardner
Source: Canadian Pacific Railway Archives, A.6200

Table of Contents

INTRODUCTION

Advertising is …

any advertiser-

controlled message,

communicated in

any media, with the

intent to influence

perception and/or

behaviour.

ALTHOUGH advertising is essentially a commercial activity, it can also be a very potent cultural force. TV and radio commercials effortlessly convey the moral principles, social values, traditions and lifestyles of a culture to itself and to others. Everyday Canadian life is played out every day in 30 and 60 second installments. Occasionally, a commercial captures the essence and imagination of a nation, and assumes iconic proportions, as happened with Molson's *I Am Canadian* "Rant"…. Sometimes they simply touch the heart in a very special Canadian way, as in Bell Canada's depiction of a young man phoning his grandfather back home in Canada from Dieppe, 'just to say thanks.'

– Association of Canadian Advertisers

In the 21st century, it is difficult to imagine a world without advertising. Both in the home and out, we are bombarded with literally thousands of images selling products and ideas. Since advertisements are such a pervasive influence in our daily lives, they have become important primary source documents for historians.

The aim of all advertising is to sell products and services, ideas and concepts. A successful advertiser is a keen observer of society, able to read and understand the mood of the time and to create a message that best reflects this mood. Therefore, in many ways, advertisements can reveal much about a society, its culture and values.

However, it is important to remember that a key element of advertising is the creation of wants and the perception of needs. Successful advertisers are able to generate in consumers a desire for the products they wish to sell. Taken in this context, advertisements are not necessarily a mirror of our everyday reality since they also project values that have been created and promoted by the marketers themselves.

When advertising first appeared in Canada in the latter part of the 19th century, it was viewed with skepticism by the business community. Few realized its potential as a marketing tool. The first advertisements were for patented medicines and household goods. Herbal remedy producers were among the earliest newspaper advertisers. This is logical, since there were few doctors, and families had to use remedies found in the home.

By 1901, Canada's population was over 5 million. It was producing vast quantities of primary goods for export to the world market, including timber and wheat. New cities were developing as manufacturing centres all across the country, from Vancouver and Winnipeg in the west to Saint John and Halifax in the east. The cities grew at a phenomenal rate, doubling and tripling in size over a number of years. The construction of the railway facilitated communications and the transportation of people and goods across the country. Canadians were able to harness and profit from their natural resources.

As the primary channel of advertising, daily newspaper circulation rose dramatically. At the turn of the century there were 97 dailies with a total circulation of 400 000. By 1940, with a population of over 11 million, there were approximately 100 dailies with a total circulation of over 2 million. Today, ads fill more than 60% of any newspaper. The percentage is even higher with magazines.

Manufacturers quickly understood the power of advertising. The growth in newspaper readership led to the development of the repeat ad: advertisers ran the same ads regularly so that potential customers became familiar with their products. It was soon evident that purchasing patterns were linked to product identification. Upon entering a store, customers invariably purchased products with which they had been made familiar. Advertising worked… as it still does today.

Through the 20th century, advertising

images and the media vehicles that carry them have become ever more sophisticated as technology developed. By 1910, ads were found in newspapers and periodicals, on billboards, in catalogues (the Eaton's catalogue had already become a Canadian icon), and in many other printed materials. Advertising moved to the radio in the 1920s and television in the 1950s. Over the next three decades, ads were sent via direct mail, the telephone, and the fax machine. Junk mail and telephone/fax solicitations became constant irritations for many. By the end of the 1990s, the Internet had become the newest significant vehicle for advertisers, and ads were introduced in movie theatres — feature films are now preceded by dozens of advertisements.

The powerful effect of advertising on societal trends was evident as early as the 1920s. Tobacco companies, for example, sought to increase their consumer base by targeting women and encouraging them to smoke. Men were sold the idea that a machine-made suit was as good as a tailor-made suit. During the two World Wars, the government launched successful campaigns to win public support for the war effort.

As they were invented, household items such as stoves, furnaces, vacuum cleaners, washers and dryers, and air-conditioners, were advertised extensively and became household necessities. In the 1950s, when consumer spending was needed to revive the post-war economy, the modern home-owner became a major advertising target.

From the carriage to the bicycle to the automobile, consumers have long been sold the message that the newest and best vehicle would improve their quality of life. In the early 1900s, ads moved from selling bicycles to promoting the new automobiles. By 1936, despite the Depression, there were 16 automotive assembly plants in Canada. In the 1950s, car sales skyrocketed. As the business grew, so did the connection between the sale of cars and advertising. Lifestyle, social standing, and personal image became interconnected with the model of car that one owned.

Phonographs were introduced at the turn of the century. By 1911, there were regular ads selling records. Radios became the norm in the 1920s, and by 1939, Canadians owned approximately 1.5 million radio sets. Advertising became an important means of funding radio productions and stations.

Moving pictures were launched at the Chicago World's Fair in the late 19th century. By the 1920s, audiences were flocking to the theatres to watch motion pictures with stars like Charlie Chaplin and Mary Pickford. Bombarded by ads featuring glamorous movie images, the public became ever more enamored with Hollywood.

By the late 20th century, new technology dramatically changed the way we live. Through widespread advertising, the computer, palm pilot, and cell phone have become necessities in business and even at home and in school.

The demographic makeup of the population is a vital consideration for advertisers. By 2000, young adolescents, who represent a multi-billion dollar market, have become the focus of advertisers. Fifty-nine percent of Canada's teenagers have a bank account and 20% have an automated banking machine card. Therefore food, clothing and entertainment ads are geared to this new financially strong group, through advertising via traditional and new channels like the Internet, cell phones, bank machines, and even within the classroom.

Finally, it is important to recognize the role of American advertising images in our society. At the turn of the century, 100 manufacturers in Canada were controlled or affiliated with American firms. By 1934 that number had increased to 1 350. Today, Canada does 85% of its trade with the United States, and American companies own or control the majority of Canadian businesses. There has always been a uniquely "Canadian" market, however, and advertisers understand that what works in the United States might not necessarily sell in Canada. Therefore, manufacturers often hire two advertising firms: one American and one Canadian.

The advertisements presented in this collection have been selected from a wide variety of print sources. Various themes such as evolving technology and changes in fashion can be seen throughout the book. Social trends are also evident in the changing attitudes towards, messages about, and representation of gender roles, minority ethnic groups, the physically and mentally challenged, and the aged.

From our modern perspective, historical advertisements are often humorous, sometimes silly or even quite shocking. Examining the reasons behind this can be enlightening. Is it the language or the message that is outdated or inappropriate within our 21st century context? Have products and/or people changed to reflect different values or interests? A comparison of advertisements from each decade of the 20th century can speak volumes about the evolving interests and values of the public, as well as the development of Canadian culture. Advertisements are a fun and valuable springboard for historical study. ❏

1900 - 1909

1889	1896
First ad agency established: A.McKim & Co., Newspaper Advertising Agency	Sir Wilfred Laurier (Liberal) becomes Prime Minister

At the beginning of the 20th century, Canada was evolving from a mainly rural, agricultural and small-town nation into an urban, manufacturing country. The small, locally oriented cottage industries were disappearing and were being replaced by large, centralized factories producing goods such as furniture, clothing, shoes, canned goods, and processed foods. Foundries and mills were expanding; factories were powered by steam and electricity; and the telegraph was becoming a common communication channel.

At this time, many people shopped at the General Store, particularly in rural areas. However, the concept of the large, urban department store was rapidly developing. By the beginning of the 20th century, Eaton's was already a Canadian icon, its catalogue reaching people right across the country.

By 1910, the majority of Canadians had moved into the cities and Canada was no longer predominantly a nation of farmers. The city had many attractions — job choices, steady wages, services, and entertainment. The two major urban centres were Montreal and Toronto.

Canadians were occupied with questions about imperialism, nationalism, and identity. Women and labour groups formed organizations to improve rights and conditions, especially in the cities where housing, health care, and education were under considerable strain. This marked the end of the Victorian period that sought to retain the controlled moral environment of the past.

Advertisements throughout this period revealed a commitment to the new religion of the time: science. Science and technology played a major role in redefining society, and the prominent social reformers of the period utilized science to justify their actions. Advertisements featured new products that promised to improve the lives of Canadians as well as take them into the modern age.

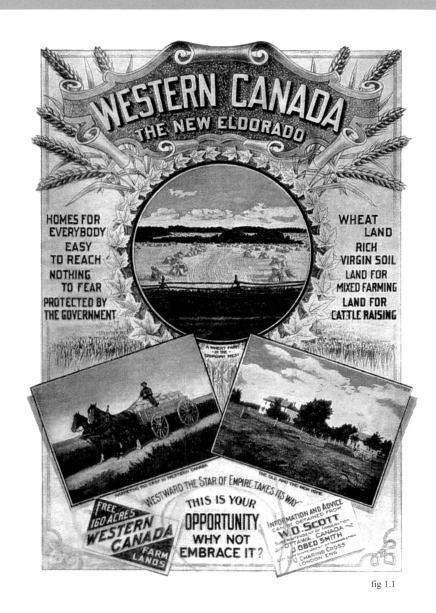

fig 1.1

Eaton's Special Settler's Catalogue, 1903

Have you tried Eaton's Mail Order System?
Most people have. If you have lived in Canada any length of time in all probability you have and are using it to-day. If you and we are strangers we want to get acquainted with one another, that is why we send you this little catalogue. In compiling this booklet one of the objects kept in view is that of giving useful and accurate information to the new Settlers and home Seekers in the Great Canadian North West. To them the store's usefulness knows no limit. It provides every possible need for furnishing the home from cellar to attic; its stocks embrace every Household Help and also includes wearing apparel of every reliable kind for man, woman and child. The distance need be no barrier for the Eaton Mail Order system extends to every Town, Village and Post Office in the Dominion of Canada from the Yukon to Nova Scotia. This store is to Canada what Montgomery Ward of Sears Roebuck is to the United States.

TOY DRUM

18-147. Toy Drum with a good tone, sheepskin and fibre heads, 8 inches in diameter, brightly lithographed with Canadian emblem. Complete with two drum sticks. Price......... **49c**

fig 1.2

1899	1900	1901	1902
Canadian National Railway is incorporated	Wireless radio invented by Reginald Fessenden in 1900	The first wireless message is transmitted across the Atlantic and received on Signal Hill, Newfoundland	The Victor Company produces first radio

1900
–
1909

fig 1.3

We do Half Your Washing Free of Cost

Text from ad:

We do Half Your Washing Free of Cost

You must pay the washer-woman fifteen cents an hour.

It is hard-earned money at that. If you do your own washing, or have the servant do it, this steaming, back-breaking, hand-chapping, cold catching, temper-destroying work will cost you more than 15 cents an hour in the end.

It takes eight hours hard labor to do the average family wash.

Eight hours, at 15 cents, costs you $1.20 per week for washing.

This means $62.40 per year, without reckoning fuel for fires, or wear on clothes.

We will save you half of that - or No Pay.

We will send any reliable person our "1900 Junior" Washing Machine on a full month's free trial.

It runs on ball bearings like a bicycle, and it works with motor-springs.

These motor-springs do most of the hard work.

You can sit in a rocking chair and make them do the washing – think of that!

We don't want a cent of your money, nor a note, nor a contract, when we ship you the Washer on trial. We even pay all of the freight out of our own pockets, so that you may test the machine as much as you like before you agree to buy it.

Use it a full month at our expense. If you don't find it does better washing in half the time – send it back to the railway station, with our address on it – that's all.

We will then pay the freight back, too, without a murmur.

But, if the month's test convinces you that our "1900 Junior" Washer actually does 8 hours washing in 4 hours time – does it twice as easy – far better, without wearing the clothes, breaking a button, or tearing a thread of lace, then you must write and tell us so.

• • • •

From that time on you must pay us, every week, part of what our machine saves you, say 50 cents per week till the Washer is paid for.

Each "1900 Junior" Washer lasts at least five years, yet a very few months, at 50 cents a week, makes it entirely your own, out of what it saves you on each washing.

Every year our Washer will save you about $31.20 that you would have had to spent for labor of your own, or the labor of others.

In five years each machine saves its owner about $136.00. Yet the "1900 Junior" Washer won't cost you a cent, under our plan, because we let it pay for itself.

You need not take our word for that. We let you prove all we say, at our expense, before you decide to buy it on these terms.

Could we risk the freight both ways, with thousands of people, if we did not know our "1900 Junior" Washer would do all we claim for it?

It costs you only the two-cent stamp, on a letter to us, to bring this quick and easy Washer to your door, on a month's trial.

That month's free use of it will save you about $2.00. You thus risk nothing but the postage stamp to prove our claims, and we practically pay you $2.00 to try it.

This offer may be withdrawn at any time if it crowds our factory.

Therefore WRITE TODAY, while the offer is open, and while you think of it. A post card will do.

Address me personally for this offer, via:

J V Bach, Manager "1900" Washer Co., 355 Yonge Street, Toronto, Ont.

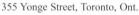

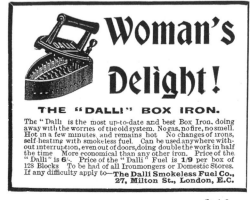

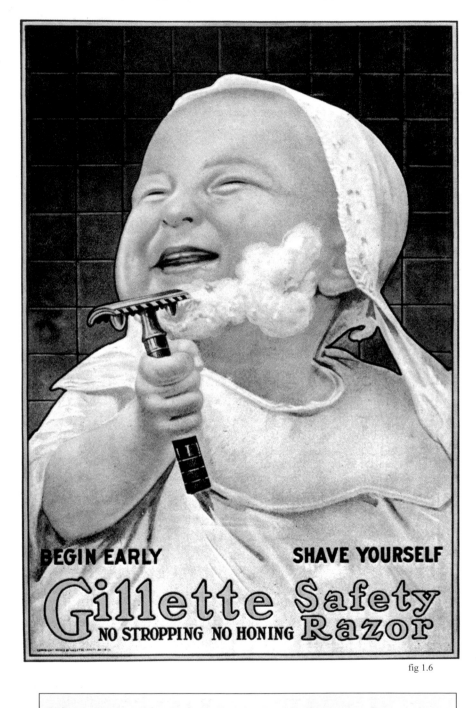

BEGIN EARLY   SHAVE YOURSELF

Gillette Safety Razor
NO STROPPING NO HONING

fig 1.6

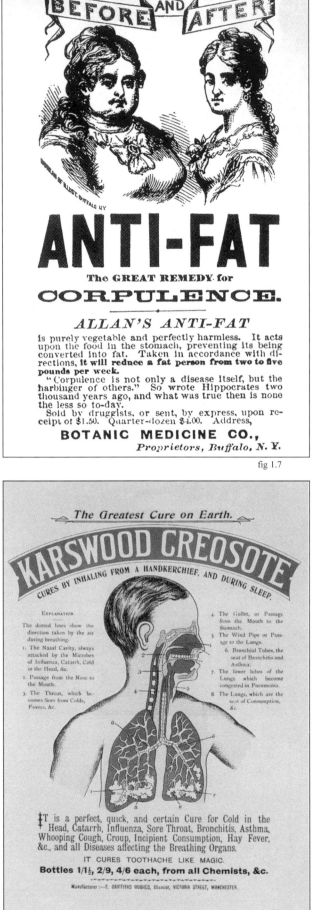

BEFORE AND AFTER

ANTI-FAT

The GREAT REMEDY for

CORPULENCE.

ALLAN'S ANTI-FAT

is purely vegetable and perfectly harmless. It acts upon the food in the stomach, preventing its being converted into fat. Taken in accordance with directions, **it will reduce a fat person from two to five pounds per week.**

"Corpulence is not only a disease itself, but the harbinger of others." So wrote Hippocrates two thousand years ago, and what was true then is none the less so to-day.

Sold by druggists, or sent, by express, upon receipt of $1.50. Quarter-dozen $4.00. Address,

BOTANIC MEDICINE CO.,

Proprietors, Buffalo, N. Y.

fig 1.7

The Greatest Cure on Earth.

KARSWOOD CREOSOTE

CURES BY INHALING FROM A HANDKERCHIEF, AND DURING SLEEP.

EXPLANATION

The dotted lines show the direction taken by the air during breathing.
1. The Nasal Cavity, always attacked by the Microbes of Influenza, Catarrh, Cold in the Head, &c.
2. Passage from the Nose to the Mouth.
3. The Throat, which becomes Sore from Colds, Fevers, &c.

4. The Gullet, or Passage from the Mouth to the Stomach.
5. The Wind Pipe or Passage to the Lungs.
6. Bronchial Tubes, the seat of Bronchitis and Asthma.
7. The lower lobes of the Lungs which become congested in Pneumonia.
8. The Lungs, which are the seat of Consumption, &c.

‡IT is a perfect, quick, and certain Cure for Cold in the Head, Catarrh, Influenza, Sore Throat, Bronchitis, Asthma, Whooping Cough, Croup, Incipient Consumption, Hay Fever, &c., and all Diseases affecting the Breathing Organs.

IT CURES TOOTHACHE LIKE MAGIC.

Bottles 1/1½, 2/9, 4/6 each, from all Chemists, &c.

Manufacturer—E. GRIFFITHS HUGHES, Chemist, VICTORIA STREET, MANCHESTER.

fig 1.9

The Globe, Toronto, Friday April 3 1903

HELP WANTED

Flour packer wanted – an experienced flour packer – must be strong, active man – well recommended. Apply with references.

Wanted – laundrymaid – to assist in housework where the other servants are kept.

Dressmakers and sewing girls wanted – will furnish information about cutting and fitting free for asking.

A good plain cook wanted – highest wages.

Wanted – a smart young man – one who understands the gum and cream work; must be steady and sober.

SITUATIONS WANTED

Good alround chef (english) wants job in or out of the city.

Boy with wheel desires work.

fig 1.8

1907	1908	1908	1909
Canada Dry Ginger Ale invented by John A. McLaughlin	Sam McLaughlin produces assembly line automobiles in Canada	Lucy M. Montgomery publishes her novel: *Anne of Green Gables*	Canada and the United States form an International Joint Commission on trade

1900 – 1909

fig 1.10

fig 1.11

fig 1.13

fig 1.12

fig 1.14

1910 - 1919

1911

Robert Borden (Conservative)
becomes Prime Minister

1911

The Boundaries of Manitoba,
Ontario and Quebec are extended

In the second decade of the 20th century, Canadians participated in a major world war that would change them both domestically and internationally. Canada's involvement in the war was substantial and resulted in many losses: 170 000 injured, 50 000 deaths, billions of dollars in costs, and 50 000 more deaths in the influenza epidemic that followed the end of the war.

The war created major rifts between French and English Canadians over the quality and quantity of support for involvement in a foreign war. Women participated massively in the workforce, replacing men in factory jobs not previously open to women, in munitions and aircraft plants. As well, women were beginning to win the right to vote federally and provincially, except in Quebec.

A major government advertising campaign encouraged Canadians to participate in the war effort by enlisting, by supporting the increasing taxes (including the new, "temporary" income tax), by rationing food consumption, and by purchasing war bonds. Commercial ads during this time also encouraged patriotic sentiment and products were often connected to the war effort. As well, technological advances, originally aimed at creating better war products, led to the development of new consumer products that improved the lives of Canadians.

On August 19, 1914, the Association of Canadian Advertisers was founded by advertising managers from eleven major international companies: Best Foods, Cadbury Beverages, Esso Petroleum, Ford, General Motors, Gillette, Goodyear Tire and Rubber Company, Kodak, Lever Brothers, Nabisco Brands, and the Royal Bank. Troubled by the condition of the advertising industry in Canada at that time, these advertising managers discussed ways to control false advertising claims made by some companies. Copy for one ad, for example, proclaimed the product could cure measles in one week, scarlet fever in two, and cancer in three!

fig 2.1

fig 2.2

fig 2.3

1913	1913	1914	1914
Zipper invented by Gideon Sundback	Over 400 000 immigrants arrive in Canada	Canada enters World War I	The Association of Canadian Advertisers is established

1910
–
1919

fig 2.4

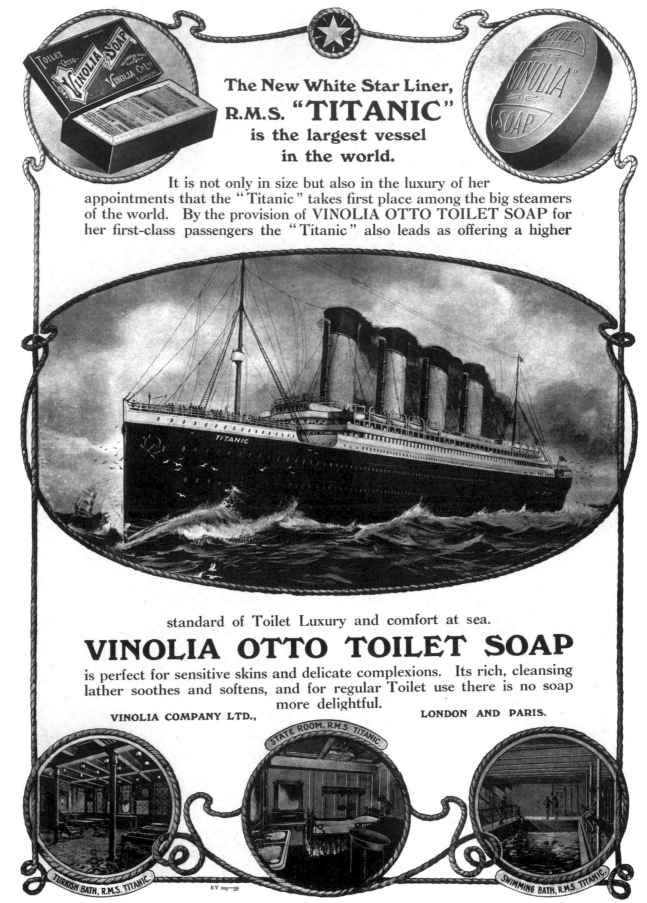

The New White Star Liner, R.M.S. "TITANIC" is the largest vessel in the world.

It is not only in size but also in the luxury of her appointments that the "Titanic" takes first place among the big steamers of the world. By the provision of VINOLIA OTTO TOILET SOAP for her first-class passengers the "Titanic" also leads as offering a higher

standard of Toilet Luxury and comfort at sea.

VINOLIA OTTO TOILET SOAP

is perfect for sensitive skins and delicate complexions. Its rich, cleansing lather soothes and softens, and for regular Toilet use there is no soap more delightful.

VINOLIA COMPANY LTD.,   LONDON AND PARIS.

Vinolia Otto Toilet Soap. Ad. 1912. Vinolia Company Ltd   fig 2.5

fig 2.6

fig 2.7

fig 2.8

1918	1918	1919	1919
Women gain right to vote federally	Federal government introduces Prohibition	Arthur Meighen (Conservative) becomes Prime Minister	Short wave radio invented

1910
–
1919

BUILDINGS

Size 22 ft. by 16 ft.

centres. The
o. 3 fir drop
lined with
all plate.

l construct-
able is well
0, 9 lights.

eight

.... 147.15

aper

.... 15.40

.... 13.45

.... 176.00

fig 2.9

CURVES OF YOUTH

will be yours if you will

"Pull the Cords"

Gives the
Flesh the
Resiliency
and
Freshness
of
Youth

Prevents
Double
Chins

Effaces
Double
Chins

PROF.
MACK'S

Chin Reducer
and
Beautifier

Reduces
Enlarged
Glands

The only mechanism producing a concentrated, continuous massage of the chin and neck, dispelling flabbiness of the neck and throat, restoring a rounded contour to thin, scrawny necks and faces, bringing a natural, healthy color to the cheeks, effacing lines and wrinkles. Price only $10. What better investment could be made? Sent postpaid immediately.

Free Booklet

—giving valuable information on how to treat double chin and enhance facial beauty will be sent on request. Write at once to

Prof. Eugene Mack

507 Fifth Ave.   Suite 1004   New York

fig 2.11

1919

"On your way home from School, be sure to call at the Grocer's in New Street for my Sunlight Soap."

£1000
SUNLIGHT
SOAP
GUARANTEE OF PURITY

1969 *"On your way home from the Academy of Futurist Philosophy, be sure to call at the Store in 41st Street for my Sunlight Soap."*

Education endorses the worth of SUNLIGHT SOAP

Time cannot improve upon it.

LEVER BROTHERS LIMITED, PORT SUNLIGHT.

fig 2.10

Woman's Looks

A woman's looks count for so much more than a man's in the sum of life, that she owes it to herself to do all that she reasonably can to preserve, and if possible enhance, whatever grace and charm of person nature may have endowed her with.

To this end—

ESTABLISHED 1789

Pears' Soap

The Great English Complexion Soap

the purest and best toilet soap ever manufactured contributes in an eminent degree. Its dainty emollient action softens and refines the skin and keeps it in a healthy condition.

It is Matchless for the Complexion

"All rights secured"   OF ALL SCENTED SOAPS PEARS' OTTO OF ROSE IS THE BEST

fig 2.12

13

Aptly named the "Roaring 20s," the decade following the First World War was one that saw the loosening of social norms. After years of restraint and suffering, society was ready to have fun. Canadians began exploring alternative lifestyles through fashion, fads, and entertainment. Artists and writers explored new ideas. Jazz music and avant-garde art challenged traditions from the past.

The war and growing economic and cultural ties with the United States helped break Canada from direct ties with Britain. With a growing sense of autonomy, Canadians looked for new ways to define themselves. Their attention turned southwards: American publications, movies, and products swept in.

Canadians developed a new international recognition through their membership in the League of Nations and women gained further rights to participate in higher government decisions with their victory in the Persons Case in 1929.

Ads reflected these exciting times by encouraging independent lifestyles and fun. In response to anti-Victorian ideals, women cut their hair and wore short skirts. All members of society questioned the traditions of the past and sought to create a special Canadian identity.

The telephone came into widespread use at this time. In the early twenties, one in four families had a telephone. By 1929, three out of four families had a telephone. In 1927, telephone connections linked Canada and Great Britain.

Radios were found in many homes during the 1920s. The Victor Radio and Phonograph Company offered consumers dozens of models in their advertisements. The radio became an important new medium through which advertisers promoted their products.

The 1920s ended with the stock market crash of 1929, a signal of an economic depression that would grip the world for most of the following decade.

fig 3.1

fig 3.2

1921	1921	1922	1924	1927
William Lyon Mackenzie King (Liberal) becomes Prime Minister	Agnes Macphail becomes the first woman elected to the House of Commons	First 3-D movie introduced	Oil is discovered in Alberta	Motorized snowblower is invented

1920
–
1929

Building Boys
IS BETTER THAN
Mending Men

Join "Your"

And Serve Humbersi...

...ristian stand...

Shooting Straight

Accurate eyes--instant response--perfect control

YMCA

SHOOTING STRAIGHT

Perfect balance of body, mind and spirit —true preparation for life's tasks, challenges and rewards. Here is thrill of achievement—comradeship and "fight" with kindred spirits.

The world gives way to the fellow who shoots straight. The man who knows where he is going—who swerves not from his path—who is ready and fit for the moment when life gives him his chance to "shoot."

Hundreds of Toronto young men are using the Y.M.C.A. to gain greater self-development, self-control and self-expression—fitting themselves to make the most of life—"Shooting Straight" to their life goals. Why not consider to-day how you, too, can use your

Y M C A

CENTRAL Y.M.C.A., 40 COLLEGE ST.

fig 3.3

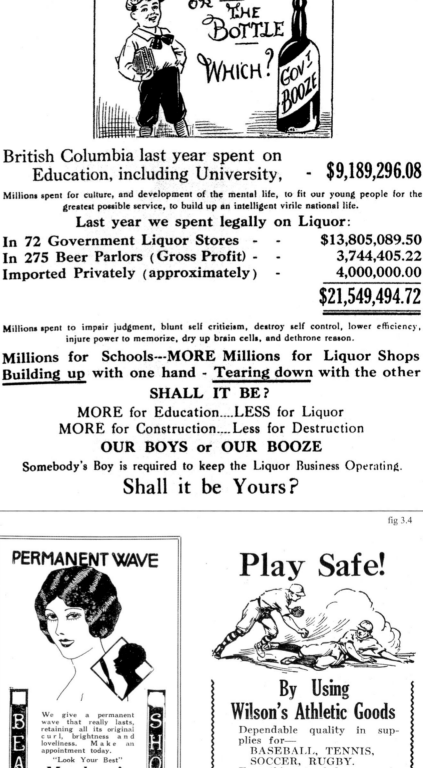

THE BOY OR THE BOTTLE WHICH?

GOV'T BOOZE

British Columbia last year spent on Education, including University, - **$9,189,296.08**

Millions spent for culture, and development of the mental life, to fit our young people for the greatest possible service, to build up an intelligent virile national life.

Last year we spent legally on Liquor:

In 72 Government Liquor Stores - -		$13,805,089.50
In 275 Beer Parlors (Gross Profit) - -		3,744,405.22
Imported Privately (approximately) -		4,000,000.00
		$21,549,494.72

Millions spent to impair judgment, blunt self criticism, destroy self control, lower efficiency, injure power to memorize, dry up brain cells, and dethrone reason.

Millions for Schools---MORE Millions for Liquor Shops
Building up with one hand - Tearing down with the other
SHALL IT BE?
MORE for Education....LESS for Liquor
MORE for Construction....Less for Destruction
OUR BOYS or OUR BOOZE
Somebody's Boy is required to keep the Liquor Business Operating.
Shall it be Yours?

fig 3.4

KING CHARLES II
received the first Pineapple grown in England

CHARLES II of England was very fond of Pineapples and quantities of them were brought for his table from the Barbados Islands in the West Indies.

He persuaded the Royal Gardener to grow the fruit in England and this was attempted. The presentation of the first Pineapple grown in England to the Stuart Monarch was made a great event.

To-day Neilson's also insist on Pineapples "good enough for a king" for use in the centres of certain of their chocolates.

The pick of the nut crops in Spain, the most luscious raisins from Australia, oranges and lemons from Sicily and other sunny lands, cherries from Italy, the finest cane sugar, whatever it is, only the best is brought to Neilson's.

Neilson's now have special arrangements with every Dealer whereby Neilson's Chocolates will be sold only while fresh, and therefore at their best.

Neilson's new low prices—60c per lb. for former $1.00 Chocolates, and 50c per lb. for former 60c Chocolates makes it an economy as well as a delight to buy them.

Neilson's
CHOCOLATES
ARE ALWAYS FRESH

Page one-hundred-seventy-seven

fig 3.5

PERMANENT WAVE

BEAUTY SHOPPE

We give a permanent wave that really lasts, retaining all its original curl, brightness and loveliness. Make an appointment today.
"Look Your Best"
Mowbray's
Hairdressing Parlor
496 Runnymede Road
Open Evenings by Appointment
PHONE LY. 2790

fig 3.6

Play Safe!

By Using Wilson's Athletic Goods

Dependable quality in supplies for—
BASEBALL, TENNIS, SOCCER, RUGBY.
Everything to help you win your game.
Catalogue on request.

The Harold A. Wilson
COMPANY LIMITED
Manufacturers of
Athletic and Sporting Goods
Gymnasium and Playground Apparatus
297-299 Yonge St., Toronto

fig 3.7

15

1927

Diamond Jubilee of Confederation;
July 1 celebration with national broadcast
linking 23 radio stations

1927

Reginald Fessenden patents an
electronic television system

1927

Ted Rogers establishes
radio station CFRB

fig 3.8

fig 3.9

fig 3.10

fig 3.11

fig 3.12

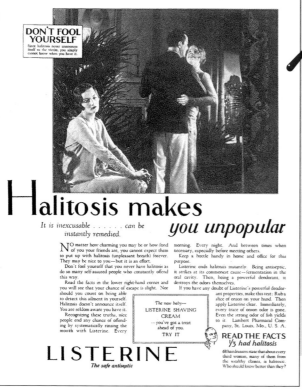

fig 3.13

 Text from ad:

HALITOSIS MAKES YOU UNPOPULAR

It is inexcusable... can be instantly remedied.

No matter how charming you may be or how fond of you your friends are, you cannot expect them to put up with halitosis (unpleasant breath) forever. They may be nice to you — but it is an effort.

Don't fool yourself that you never have halitosis as do so many self-assured people who constantly offend this way.

Read the facts in the lower right-hand corner and you will see that your chance of escape is slight. Nor should you count on being able to detect this ailment in yourself. Halitosis doesn't announce itself. You are seldom aware you have it.

Recognizing these truths, nice people end any chance of offending by systematically rinsing the mouth with Listerine. Every morning. Every night. And between times when necessary, especially before meeting others.

Keep a bottle handy in home and office for this purpose.

Listerine ends halitosis instantly. Being antiseptic, it strikes at its commonest cause — fermentation in the oral cavity. Then, being a powerful deodorant, it destroys the odors themselves.

If you have any doubt of Listerine's powerful deodorant properties, make this test: Rub a slice of onion on your hand. Then apply Listerine clear. Immediately, every trace of onion odor is gone. Even the strong odor of fish yields to it. Lambert Pharmacal Company, St.Louis, Mo., U. S. A.

READ THE FACTS
1/3 had halitosis
68 hairdressers state that about every third woman, many of them from the wealthy classes, is halitoxic. Who should know better than they?

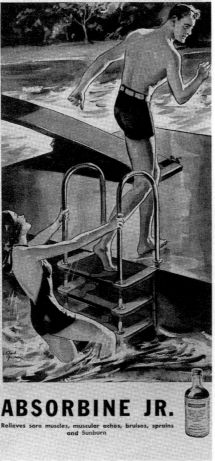

fig 3.14

fig 3.15

1930 - 1939

1930
Beginning of the
Great Depression

1930
R.B. Bennett (Conservative)
becomes Prime Minister

The 1929 Wall Street crash signalled the Great Depression in Canada that lasted for most of the decade. Unemployment ran between 25-30% so that most Canadians, even the middle class, were deeply affected. A terrible drought in the west resulted in destructive dust storms and grasshoppers that destroyed land and crops. Thousands of Canadians abandoned their farms. The cities witnessed deplorable poverty as factories closed down and the unemployed waited in long lines at the soup kitchens for food. The government responded in very limited ways. These initiatives provided little aid in the depressed state faced by most Canadians.

The ads during this time reflect a better life. Although few Canadians had any purchasing power, consumers were exposed to a wide variety of new products. Cheap prices made it possible for those with money to enjoy the new technological advances of the time.

In 1937, the Association of Canadian Advertisers initiated the formation of the Canadian Circulations Audit Board, bringing together the Canadian trade and business press publishers, advertising agencies and advertisers, to implement an effective method to audit controlled-circulation numbers of publications, that were used to determine the cost of advertising. The Canadian Association of Broadcasters approached the ACA and the Canadian Association of Advertising Agencies (now the Institute of Communications in Advertising) for help in maintaining credibility in broadcast advertising. As a result, the Bureau of Broadcast Measurement, an independent research organization under the control of the three organizations, was established in 1942.

fig 4.1

fig 4.2

1930
–
1939

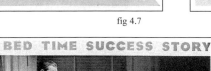

fig 4.12

21

1940 - 1949

1940	1941	1941
Canada declares war on Italy	Japanese attack Pearl Harbor; Canada declares war on Japan	Appearance of first computer controlled by software; Invention of aerosol spray cans and the neutronic reactor

In the 1940s, Canadians were once again involved in a major war. During World War II the federal government created a number of departments to mobilize support for war production and participation. Advertisers were called upon to help generate mass support for the war effort with elaborate propaganda campaigns. Victory bonds and loans, essential to funding the military effort, were widely promoted during the war years. Phrases such as "patriotic duty," images of war victims and of fighting men, as well as dehumanized images of the enemy, helped mobilize support for the war. The result was that increases in taxes and restrictions on Canadians were, for the most part, readily accepted, as Canadians saw them as necessary measures during the war.

Manufacturers were more than happy to increase production, particularly in 1939, in the aftermath of the Great Depression. Every organization and manufacturer wanted a link to the war effort to demonstrate support, boost morale, and of course, to sell more products. Many ads targeted women's role on the Home Front by emphasizing conservation, rationing, and voluntary agencies. As well, many women had entered the workforce during the war, and ads often celebrated their contributions. A highly regulated economy produced almost full employment for both men and women.

Major social reforms took place in this decade. Unemployment insurance was introduced in 1941, family allowances in 1944, and the veterans benefit packages at the end of the war. In the west, the Co-operative Commonwealth Federation (CCF) established in 1932, expanded under the leadership of Saskatchewan Premier Tommy Douglas.

The technology developed for the war effort led to the creation of modern consumer products that helped boost the post-war economy. Advertisements in the late 1940s created a demand for cars, houses, and new labour-saving appliances.

War-time Needs

To serve in Canada and Overseas
Male Stenographers and Clerks for every branch of the service.
Female Stenographers to fill vacancies resulting from enlistment and war-time industrial programs.

For information, contact

THE GREGG EMPLOYMENT SERVICE
1200 BAY STREET   -   MIdway 1107

fig 5.1

How Recruits in the know fight the Dry Scalp foe!

Once in the army it doesn't take long for sun, dust and wind...

...to dry out the scalp, make hair wild and woolly!

but...5 drops a day keeps DRY SCALP away

... MAKES 'VASELINE' HAIR TONIC FIRST WITH SERVICE MEN IN AMERICA!

It'll improve your hair, too!

Here's a cue for you! Men in the armed services, whose hair leads the hardest life of all, prefer 'Vaseline' Hair Tonic to any other brand. Think what it will do for your hair! Comb a few drops into your hair each day ... or rub directly on the scalp. Then massage vigorously with plenty of 'Vaseline' Hair Tonic before shampooing. That's all you have to do to fight Dry Scalp, keep your hair neat and well-groomed. Buy a bottle today!

DIG DOWN DEEP FOR WAR BONDS!

Vaseline HAIR TONIC 40¢ and 70¢
REG. U. S. PAT. OFF.

fig 5.2

fig 5.3

What's the Rush?

It's the telephone rush. Every night thousands of service men and women dash to the nearest telephones to talk with families and friends at home. Most of the Long Distance calls from camps and naval stations are crowded into a few short hours.

Many circuits are likely to be crowded at that time and it helps a lot when you "give 7 to 10 to the service men."

BELL TELEPHONE SYSTEM

fig 5.4

Challenge!

This is a fight to the finish. No room for half measures. No room for delay. This is urgent... vital...pressing. This is WAR.

More men, well equipped, well clothed, well fed, mean more dollars.

Canada looks to you to supply those dollars...and to keep on supplying them till this war is won.

Start saving NOW. Buy war savings certificates regularly. Build up your savings account. Be ready to enlist your dollars in this fight for human freedom and decency.

Be glad you can help so simply and so effectively.
Save for Victory.

THE ROYAL BANK OF CANADA
WAR SAVINGS PLEDGE FORMS AVAILABLE AT ALL BRANCHES

fig 5.5

fig 5.6

fig 5.7

fig 5.8

fig 5.9

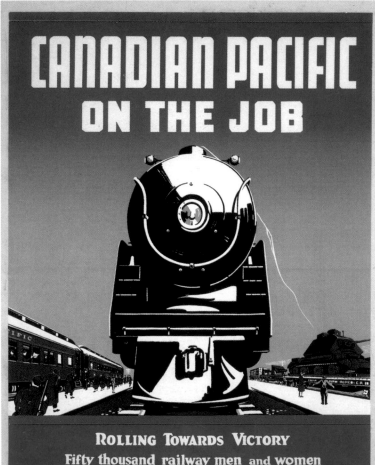

fig 5.10

fig 5.11

24

When will we have TELEVISION IN CANADA?

Imagine the day you'll sit at home in front of your first G-E television set! You'll see a bright, clear picture on the screen. It will be a *moving* picture, *with sound*. Maybe it will show you a hockey game. Maybe a musical show. Maybe a drama, or a fashion parade, or an event that is taking place on the other side of the world!

Television will bring a new pageant of entertainment right into your home. Entertainment you'll *see* and hear—as easily, as simply as you hear radio today!

For television is an accomplished fact. It was operating in England before the war. Many English people saw the Coronation in 1937, through television. They saw the Derby run. They enjoyed daily newcasts.

On this continent, too, television is in operation *now*. There are television stations in several U.S. cities. *Only the war is delaying its further development and introduction into Canada.* When peace returns and the financing can be arranged, television will come to Canada.

At first it may be available only in thickly populated areas. But scientists, partly as a result of their wartime work on secret devices, are perfecting ways of ensuring television coverage for the whole country.

In the task of equipping Canada for television, Canadian General Electric with its great resources, stands ready to play a big part—eager to hasten the day when *you* will be able to enjoy the miracle of television.

CGE-145M

CANADIAN GENERAL ELECTRIC CO. LIMITED
HEAD OFFICE — TORONTO

fig 5.12

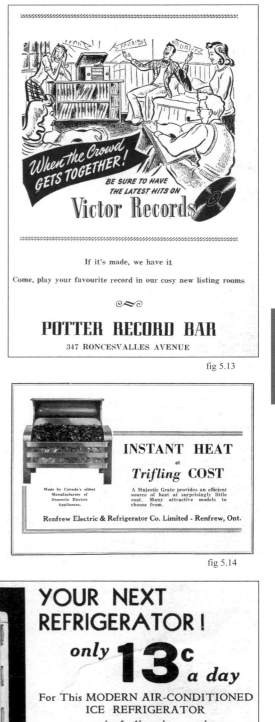

fig 5.13

fig 5.14

fig 5.15

fig 5.16

1950 - 1959

1950
Canada sends troops
to Korean War

1950
First credit card launched -
Diners Club

In the 1950s, the benefits of post-war living were glorified. In an attempt to ease the transition from soldier to civilian, post-war advertisements combined war and civilian life messages. The 1950s are synonymous with the terms baby boom, suburbia, and economic prosperity. Post-war Canada witnessed an unprecedented rise in the birth rate, coupled with a booming economy. This improvement in economic conditions, the introduction of credit cards, and the rapid development of new technology, led to a new cultural reality. Consumer purchasing power grew. Urban development was rapid. At the same time, many Canadians escaped the confines of the city for the exalted suburban life. Car sales skyrocketed, in keeping with the growing numbers who commuted into the city.

"Keeping up with the Joneses" became the mantra of the post-war generation. Advertising in this decade reflected the shift in values. Ads for consumer goods and household appliances predominated. The nuclear family and the happy housewife, epitomized by the TV sitcom "Leave it to Beaver," were the ideals represented in advertising images. Roles within the family and society were clearly defined, as were expectations for the consumer. Corporate culture was expanding. In addition to radio and print advertising, television now added a new dimension to the marketers' world. Psychology and studies of perception were increasingly used to manipulate the consumer.

Beneath this glossy surface, however, a growing unease revealed itself in the form of Cold War paranoia and in the counter-culture movement. Many began to question and rebel against the picture perfect image portrayed in ads and media stories. Just five years after WWII ended, Canadian soldiers were again sent overseas, this time to fight the growing threat of communism in Korea. The fear of nuclear Armageddon during the Cold War led to ads for bomb shelters, though this was more evident in the United States.

fig 6.1

fig 6.2

Toronto Daily Star, Friday June 29, 1951

HELP WANTED

Magazine salesman, 3 young men, 18-25 – neat appearance essential. Average – this is the fastest selling deal in existence – earnings with commission

Welders-must be thoroughly experienced -highest wages

Carpenters wanted-very steady employment – highest wages

Diemakers wanted-expanding tool shop requires 3 men who are well trained in all phases of tool room work

Furnace installers – thoroughly experienced – apply immediately

Brick and block layers-highest wages – apply immediately

fig 6.6

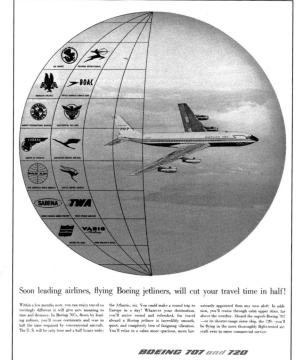

fig 6.8

THE ART OF BETTE

*Yesterday . . . Today . . . Tom
it's Electrical Living by Wes*

Let's hope it's not too far away . . . that bright new
you'll again know the lift of living electrically. A
does come, Westinghouse will be a name to rer
stands for the know-how and experience acquired
30 million pre-war electrical home appliances.

More than that . . . it stands for years of tried
background in making not just one or two appl
twenty-two different types of electrical servants for y

At the moment, we're head over heels building es
material. And we'll stick to that job until it is done
the go ahead signal flashes, you can count on We
to turn out all the fine new appliances you need

TUNE IN JOHN CHARLES THOMAS · SUNDAY 2.30 E

fig 6.9

fig 6.10

...NG

that "never done" feeling about housework. In war or peace, we take your homemaking problems to heart. The pre-war masterpieces shown above are just a promise of what's to come.

WESTINGHOUSE ELECTRIC & MANUFACTURING CO., MANSFIELD, O.
PLANTS IN 25 CITIES . . . OFFICES EVERYWHERE

30 MILLION PRE-WAR

Westinghouse

ELECTRIC HOME APPLIANCES

YOUR PROMISE OF STILL FINER ONES TO COME

AR TED MALONE • MON. WED. FRI. 10:15 EWT., BLUE NETWORK

fig 6.11

THE SOCIABLES prefer Pepsi

They entertain the modern way and they serve the modern refreshment: Pepsi-Cola. It refreshes without filling. You're one of The Sociables. Have a Pepsi anywhere — at play, at home or at your favorite soda fountain.

Pepsi-Cola

Be Sociable, Have a Pepsi

Refresh without filling

fig 6.12

Now... Have "Skin Like a baby's" in just 7 days

with pure mild Ivory! (there's magic in its mildness)

Wouldn't you like to look in your mirror and see a complexion as satin-smooth as little Cathy's? Then why not borrow her beauty soap—pure, mild Ivory! You can be sure that what Ivory does for her skin, it will do for yours!

You see, Ivory is 99 44/100% pure . . . the mildest possible beauty soap. And that Ivory mildness is complexion magic. For it protects the important inner oils that all skin needs for beauty.

Don't wait to discover what Ivory's magic mildness can do for your complexion! It's so easy. Just change to thorough cleansing with baby-gentle Ivory Soap. And you'll have a softer, lovelier complexion . . . yes, "skin like a baby's" . . . in just 7 days!

Does her flawless complexion need all kinds of special care? "No!" says this lovely model. "I have only one beauty secret—I use pure, mild Ivory daily." Shouldn't you?

4 for the price of 3!

Yes, 4 cakes of Personal Size Ivory cost about the same as 3 cakes of other well-known toilet soaps!

More doctors advise Ivory than any other soap

99 44/100% pure...it floats

IVORY Soap

fig 6.13

HUDSON'S BAY

Leisure wear

Superbly tailored men's leisure wear shirts in a wide range of authentic tartans and plain colours. Made from an exclusive lightweight 100% Pure Merino Wool fabric imported from England.

fig 6.14

29

1960 - 1969

1960

Bill of Rights passed

1961

Formation of CTV; CCF becomes NDP (New Democratic Party)

The sixties was a decade in which established traditions and ideals were challenged. Below the surface of stifling conformity of the 1950s, the Civil Rights movement and a counter-culture movement exploded around the world. In the U.S., a youthful John F. Kennedy was elected president then assassinated three years later. America became involved in the conflict in Vietnam, which led to a long war, anti-war protests, and dissension. In the U.K., the Beatles burst onto the world stage and changed popular culture forever. In Canada, Pierre Elliot Trudeau gained attention as Justice Minister. Canadian identity was given a boost when Montreal hosted Expo in 1967, in celebration of the centennial of Confederation.

Not surprisingly, advertising during this era reflected an evident shift in values, and revealed a certain liberty that had previously been unexpressed. Explosive colours and radical designs were used to express the voice of the baby boom generation, which obviously had buying power.

The family portrayed in the 1960s ad was also significantly different from that of the 1950s. Traditional values were still evident, but the 1960s family was obviously spending more time in front of the television. The timesaving TV dinner was introduced at this time. Even though the women's liberation movement was beginning to take off, many ads were still sexist in content. The man was portrayed as the breadwinner and the woman as the homemaker who needed his help and support.

The introduction of new immigration laws opened the doors to a more multicultural society, but feelings of uneasiness by traditional communities were prevalent. The 1960's also saw the development of the Parti Quebecois and the emergence of issues of separatism under the leadership of Rene Levesque.

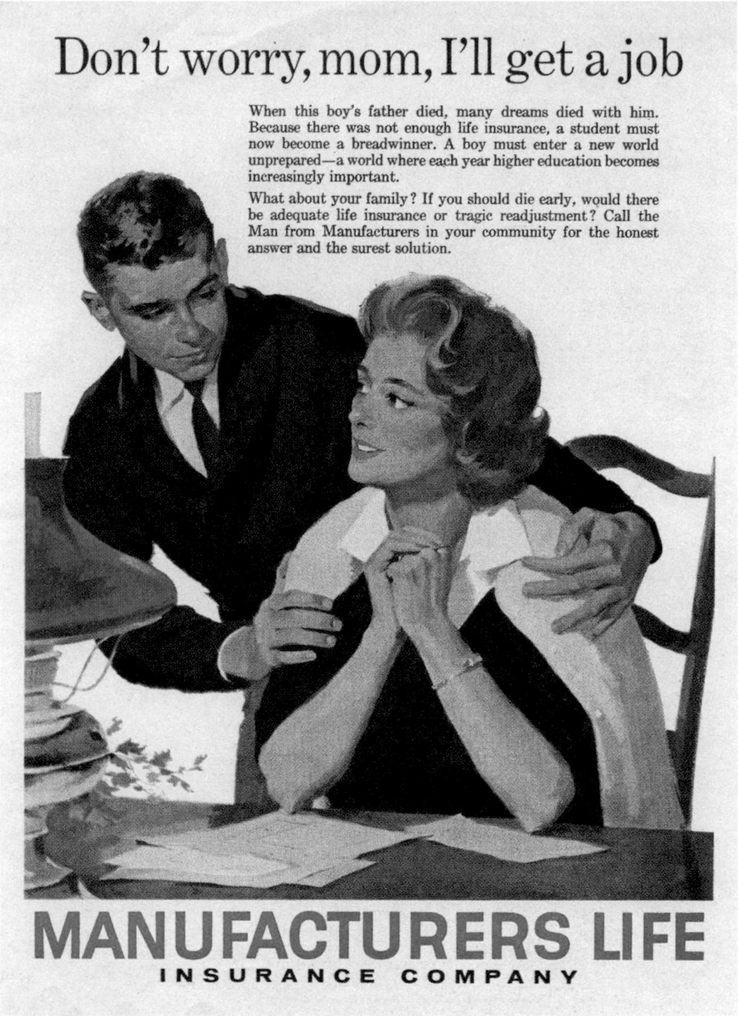

Don't worry, mom, I'll get a job
When this boy's father died, many dreams died with him. Because there was not enough life insurance, a student must now become a breadwinner. A boy must enter a new world unprepared—a world where each year higher education becomes increasingly important.
What about your family? If you should die early, would there be adequate life insurance or tragic readjustment? Call the Man from Manufacturers in your community for the honest answer and the surest solution.
MANUFACTURERS LIFE
INSURANCE COMPANY

fig 7.1

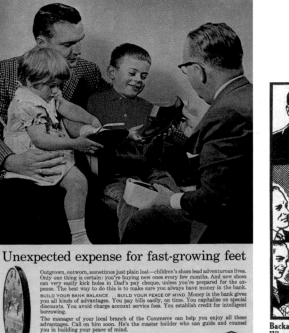

Unexpected expense for fast-growing feet
Outgrown, outworn, sometimes just plain lost—children's shoes lead adventurous lives. Only one thing is certain: you're buying new ones every few months. And new shoes can very easily kick holes in Dad's pay cheque, unless you're prepared for the expense. The best way to do this is to make sure you always have money in the bank.
BUILD YOUR BANK BALANCE . . . BUILD YOUR PEACE OF MIND. Money in the bank gives you all kinds of advantages. You pay bills easily, on time. You capitalize on special discounts. You avoid charge account service fees. You establish credit for intelligent borrowing.
The manager of your local branch of the Commerce can help you enjoy all these advantages. Call on him soon. He's the master builder who can guide and counsel you in building your peace of mind.
CANADIAN IMPERIAL
BANK OF COMMERCE
THE BANK THAT BUILDS
Over 1200 branches to serve you

fig 7.2

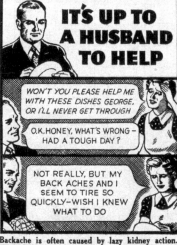

IT'S UP TO A HUSBAND TO HELP
WON'T YOU PLEASE HELP ME WITH THESE DISHES GEORGE, OR I'LL NEVER GET THROUGH
O.K. HONEY, WHAT'S WRONG – HAD A TOUGH DAY?
NOT REALLY, BUT MY BACK ACHES AND I SEEM TO TIRE SO QUICKLY–WISH I KNEW WHAT TO DO
Backache is often caused by lazy kidney action. When kidneys get out of order, excess acids and wastes remain in the system. Then backache, disturbed rest or that tired-out and heavy-headed feeling may soon follow. That's the time to take Dodd's Kidney Pills. Dodd's stimulate the kidneys to normal action. Then you feel better—sleep better—work better. Get Dodd's Kidney Pills now.

fig 7.3

Colour me Wild!

A Hot Pink here. A True Blue there. And Avocado Flips for Bold Gold. Kleenex Boutique Facial Tissues add sassy splashes of deep colour everywhere you want them. Perfumed puffs of bold colour pop out of name-dropping skinny-mini boxes. Wild ! Match them with Kleenex Boutique Bathroom Tissues and you've got a pretty wild Kleenex Boutique Collection.

Kleenex Boutique Collection

Kleenex is a reg. trade mark of Kimberly-Clark of Canada Limited

NOVEMBER 1968

Now you can do approximately 98% of your personal banking, and get cash whenever you want it, day or night, weekday or holiday.

The ROYAL BANK introduces

bankette®

the "automatic teller window"

fig 7.4

fig 7.5

CONFIDENCE
BRAND
NAMES
SATISFACTION

Practical folks buy Brand Name products

Why do you buy Brand Names? Because you trust them. You know that they are consistently good, that they always meet the high standards of quality you've set for yourself and your family. You'll find Brand Name products wherever you go. No guesswork shopping. Like good friends, they're always there.

The Brand Name manufacturer has built a reputation. He must maintain it, so he keeps his standards high, and strives constantly to make his product better. He's always first with new products and ideas. He employs lots of people. He helps balance the economy. You depend on him. He depends on you. Know your brands, and buy the brands you know. You'll find some of them on the pages of this magazine.

A Brand Name is a maker's reputation

LIBERTY MAGAZINE In Cooperation With BRAND NAMES FOUNDATION Incorporated

November, 1961

fig 7.6

Easy-to-use movie camera
New from Kodak LESS THAN $40

This year catch all the action with the KODAK 8 Movie Camera

The whole family can take movies with this new Kodak camera. There's no need to focus. Only one simple setting is required ... then just aim and shoot! It's easy to load, too! But best of all it's yours at a remarkably low price! See the new KODAK 8 Movie Camera, f/1.9 at your dealer's now ... less than $40. Price is subject to change without notice.

CANADIAN KODAK CO., LIMITED, Toronto 15, Ontario

Kodak

fig 7.7

now it's Pepsi-for those who **think young**

Thinking young is a wholesome attitude, an enthusiastic outlook. It means getting the most out of life, and everyone can join in. This is the life for Pepsi —light, bracing, clean-tasting Pepsi. Think young. Say "Pepsi, please!"

fig 7.8

A New World of Worth
from CHEVROLET

fig 7.9

INTRODUCING THE 1962 DODGE
a new lean breed of Dodge that'll out-run, out-corner and out-economize most any car around. It's undoubtedly the quickest, toughest most dependable car Dodge ever built. It's a low price, full size car . . . a thoroughbred that doesn't need pampering. It drives twice as far between oil changes, 32,000 miles between grease jobs. Its brakes adjust themselves automatically. It accelerates quicker, yet gets five per cent more miles per gallon than the '61 Dodge. The body is rustproofed . . . gives you years of high trade-in value. Want more? Dodge gives you more! Things like an improved gearshift for smoother, crisper shifts; a smaller transmission hump that gives the man in the middle more legroom; easier, more responsive steering; deep-sprung chair-high seats; to name just a few. There's never been a Dodge like this one. There's never been *any car* like this one. Drive it. You'll find it's a very, very hot automobile indeed. **DRIVE THE NEW LEAN BREED OF DODGE**
ON DISPLAY NOW AT YOUR DEPENDABLE DODGE-VALIANT DEALER

fig 7.10

Who needs extra iron— you or your mini-daughter?

Both of you have extra iron needs. This is clearly stated in the Dietary Standard for Canadians. You need 60% more iron than the most active man every day because of menstrual loss. Your daughter needs 100% more iron than a man every day due to the menstrual loss she shares with you and because she's still in her vital growing years.

Also, both of you may skimp on certain foods, and occasionally diet which might mean that you're not getting all the iron and vitamins you should have. In that case, each ONE-A-DAY* (Brand) Multiple Vitamins Plus Iron pill will provide you with eight of the essential vitamins to help you maintain your good health — plus the extra iron you and your mini-daughter need. The whole bit in one little pill. Ask for it at your Drug Store.

One-A-Day Plus Iron—to help maintain your good health.

*"One-A-Day" is a registered trademark of Miles Laboratories, Ltd.

fig 7.13

fig 7.14

You're **years ahead** with Tilden

Background from the James collection of early Canadiana

Envy will get him nowhere
...but a phone call to TILDEN will get *you* a new Chevrolet or Pontiac next time *your* car is in for repairs. With 187 locations across Canada, and world-wide affiliates (in the U.S. it's National Car Rentals) you need never be stuck for a car! There's a TILDEN station at all

Canadian airports and near all main railway terminals. TILDEN has more locations and more *new* cars than any other system in the country.

TILDEN
the CANADIAN name in world-wide car rentals

SYSTEM HEAD OFFICE: 1194 STANLEY STREET, MONTREAL

fig 7.11

Some Volkswagen owners look down on other Volkswagen owners.

When you graduate from a Volkswagen Sedan to a Volkswagen Station Wagon, you really step up in the world.

The Station Wagon stands a good foot taller than other cars.

And it holds more than the biggest conventional wagon you can find.

But the VW Wagon isn't only tall.

It's also short.

We saved 4 feet of hood in front by putting the engine in back.

Big as it is inside, it's only 9 inches longer than the Volkswagen Sedan.

So people who move up to the high-slung model still feel very much at home.

They park in the same little spots.

They still don't worry about freezing or boiling; the engine is air-cooled.

They still go a long way on a gallon of gas (about 24 miles) and a very long way on a set of tires (about 30,000 miles).

And it just tickles them to drive one Volkswagen and look down on a million others.

fig 7.12

The Chic way to get into a dress.

Chic zippers. In a rainbow of colours. The only zippers colour-matched with thread —co-ordinated by shade number with famous Coats Super Sheen thread. Slim, light and flexible, Chic zippers give you fabric-backed comfort. And a non-metallic, polyester

still rugged enough to give you years of trouble-free wear. Chic zippers. Easy to work with, chic to wear. Achieve that professional, finished look in your garments. Use colour co-ordinated Chic zippers and Coats Super Sheen thread—sew to be sure.

Chic ZIPPERS

Coats
the thread makers

fig 7.15

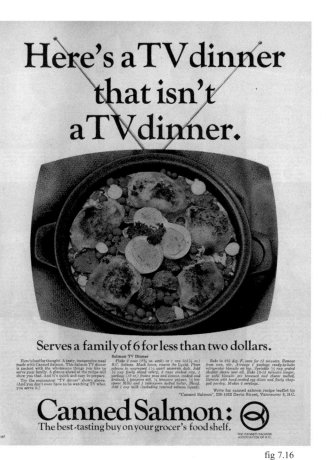

Here's a TV dinner that isn't a TV dinner.

Serves a family of 6 for less than two dollars.

Salmon TV Dinner
Flake 1 can (7½ oz. each) or 1 can (15½ oz.) B.C. Salmon. Mash loose, reserve the liquid. Place salmon in ungreased 1½ quart casserole dish. Add ½ cup finely sliced celery, 2 cups cooked rice, 1 package (10 oz.) frozen peas and onions, cooked and drained; 1 teaspoon salt, ¼ teaspoon pepper, ¼ teaspoon MSG and 1 tablespoon melted butter. Blend. Add 1 cup milk (including reserved salmon liquid).

Here's food for thought. A tasty, inexpensive meal made with Canned Salmon. This Salmon TV dinner is packed with the wholesome things you like to serve your family. A glance ahead at the recipe will show you that. And it's quick and easy to prepare. Try the economical "TV dinner" shown above. (And you don't even have to be watching TV when you serve it.)

Bake in 375 deg. F. oven for 15 minutes. Remove from oven, stir. Arrange 1 package ready-to-bake refrigerator biscuits on top. Sprinkle ½ cup grated cheddar cheese over all. Bake 15-15 minutes longer, or until biscuits are browned and cheese melted. Garnish with hard-cooked egg slices and finely chopped parsley. Makes 6 servings.

Write for canned salmon recipe leaflet to: "Canned Salmon", 736-1052 Davie Street, Vancouver 8, B.C.

Canned Salmon:
The best-tasting buy on your grocer's food shelf.

THE CANNED SALMON ASSOCIATION OF B.C.

fig 7.16

Stop missing out on
Take 7 Records for only $1.87
plus your first selection FREE
if you agree to buy only eight more during the next year at the regular Club price from hundreds to be offered.

BEGINNING THIS HOLIDAY SEASON

fig 7.17

BE RIGHT WHEN YOU WRITE

The addresses on each letter and parcel should show

■ the full name of the person who is to get it.

■ the correct apartment number, street address, rural route number or post office box number.

■ City, town or village, and postal zone number, where necessary.

■ your name and complete return address in the upper left-hand corner.

A correct postal address speeds accurate delivery

PO-61-ST

CANADA POST OFFICE

55

1960 – 1969

fig 7.18

33

1970 - 1979

1970
Hudson's Bay Company
marks 300th anniversary

1971
Greenpeace is founded

Crisis and change characterized the 1970s in Canada. Following the momentum of the radical social movements in the sixties, the women's movement continued to gain in influence through the second wave of feminism. New publications appeared giving voice to women's issues. Demonstrations and marches demanding equal rights were a regular occurrence.

The 1970s also saw the spectacular rise of one of Canada's great icons and political intellectuals: Pierre Trudeau. As Justice Minister in the late 1960s, Trudeau had already shaken the system by introducing revolutionary changes to Canadian law. As Prime Minister in October 1970 he continued to create controversy in Canada when he invoked the War Measures Act in response to the FLQ crisis in Quebec. The very force of nationalism in its most extreme form would test the will of Pierre Trudeau and the strength of Canadian unity. However, in 1972, Canadian nationalism was very much in evidence when Paul Henderson scored the unforgettable winning goal in the Canadian-Russian struggle for hockey superiority.

Popular culture of the early 1970s was greatly influenced by the hippie movement and in the latter part of the decade by disco. These trends influenced advertising images that were used to cater to and influence this new generation. As more women joined the work force and women's buying power increased, advertisers realized they had to reflect the shift in values resulting from the second wave of the feminist movement. A change in the portrayal of men and women in advertisements began to emerge. As well, banks, automobile makers, and other corporations began to target women as independent decision makers in their ads. Nevertheless, traditional stereotypes of men and women persisted in much of popular advertising.

The Chevy Monza sports a nice little figure in more ways than one.

Yes indeed, the 1980 Chevy Monza's got it all. Comfort and style, plus a way of making you feel excited about the prospect of driving from point A to point B. And at a figure that's not going to hamper your sense of practicality. Its sleek aerodynamic look invites you to hop right in and fire it up. But once inside, you'll notice standard features that are almost too good to be true. Like high-back bucket seats, a cushioned rimmed steering wheel, standard AM radio, a 4-cylinder engine, tinted glass, wall-to-wall carpeting, body side mouldings, bumper guards, hatchback convenience and believe it, even more. You've got to hand it to Chevrolet for figuring out how to get you a sporty little car packed with all the things you want. And at a price we think will figure very nicely into your idea of what a sporty little car should cost.

New vehicle warranty 12 months/20,000 kilometres. 3-yr. perforation from corrosion warranty. Available Continuous Protection Plan Option.

That's My Chevy

fig 8.1

The Halifax Chronicle Herald:
June 1, 1979

HELP WANTED
Wilderness youth leader-summer position working with local young people-outdoor experience required - salary negotiable - apply Pioneer Village Project, Halifax

Three telephone solicitors wanted - a pleasant telephone voice and a will to work

RNS and RNAS wanted immediately for a 72 bed accredited hospital

Hair stylists wanted – recently expanded and relocated Styles Unlimited now has chair rentals available for experienced operators.

fig 8.2

Or buy a Volkswagen.

Volkswagen makes the 3 highest mileage cars in America: the Rabbit Diesel 5-speed, Rabbit Diesel 4-speed and the Dasher Diesel.

fig 8.3

-SKI

g family

MARK II - COBRA

fig 8.4

They're pursuing rewarding careers at Bethlehem

A College Relations Representative based at our home office, Mary Kale recruits engineers and technical graduates for Bethlehem's management-training program.

Anita Parsons is involved in an environmental engineering support capacity at the Beth-Elkhorn Corp., Jenkins, Ky., a coal-mining subsidiary of Bethlehem. She monitors potential pollution sources to see that standards are met.

A Coordinator in Materiel Control at our Sparrows Point, Md., steel plant, Joann Jacobs evaluates procedures and methods used to control inventory of electrical and mechanical parts.

Vinnie Moody has completed the first phase of our management-training program, and is now receiving on-the-job training in industrial relations at our Johnstown, Pa., steel plant.

Kathleen Gearhart is a Programmer-Analyst in Bethlehem. Her duties involve programming and systems analysis in technical and engineering applications.

Valeria Fisher is Chief Chemist, Bethlehem Mines Corporation, at Johnstown, Pa. She manages the principal chemical laboratory, and supervises procedures for others.

Do you know a woman working toward a degree in engineering, chemistry, mathematics, or another technical discipline?

She may be interested in learning about the challenging career opportunities for women at Bethlehem Steel.

Information of interest to college students is available. Write: Director, College Relations, Bethlehem Steel Corporation, Bethlehem, PA 18016.

Bethlehem

fig 8.5

Bonus Savings and Personal Chequing.
Two accounts that work successfully together.

Bonus Savings and Personal Chequing are two accounts that can really help you keep up with your success.

You see, a Personal Chequing Account makes it easy to keep track of where your money is going. Every month you get an itemized statement and your cancelled cheques returned.

A Bonus Savings Account gives you more from the money you save. You get a high rate of interest which is paid into your account twice a year.

Together they make a very successful combination – just what you need for all your day-to-day banking. Bonus Savings and Personal Chequing from your neighbourhood Royal Bank.

When you succeed...we succeed.

ROYAL BANK

fig 8.6

Think of the Alberta Vacation Planner as a Welcome Mat

We'd like to send you and your family the Alberta Vacation Planner as an invitation to visit Alberta and really enjoy your vacation time when you're here.

Alberta

GET YOUR FREE COPY BY WRITING "TRAVEL ALBERTA", DEPT. C, 10255 - 104 STREET, EDMONTON, ALBERTA

fig 8.7

This is the pants outfit my husband bought me, after I had lost 50 pounds. It sure made me a hit!

My husband shamed me into losing 50 pounds.

By Rita O'Dwyer—as told to Ruth L. McCarthy.

It was a movie book in a beauty salon that finally got me to reduce. I'd gone for my weekly upsweep, though I knew I'd come home to my

about the Ayds Vitamin and Mineral Reducing Plan. I went straight to the drugstore for a box of the plain chocolate fudge-type.

fig 8.8

Behind every beautiful woman, there's a beautiful woman.

Who is she? Your Avon Lady, bringing wonderful products for you and everyone you love. She talks "beauty" with confidence and a smile, and she'll keep you smiling, too, with home service for all your cosmetic and grooming needs. Take a little time out for yourself the next time the doorbell rings and it's Avon Calling.

AVON

fig 8.9

How Roots give your feet a good feeling, then send it up your spine.

To see the idea behind Roots, take a side-view look at the shoe. Instead of a heel to lift you up and tilt you forward, you'll find a one-piece base to plant you firmly in touch with Mother Earth. Roots, you see, work very much like roots. And if you take a side-view look at the human foot, you'll see why they work as well as they do. Your heel is the lowest part of your foot, so in Roots it sits in the lowest part of your shoe.

Suddenly you stand straighter as additional muscles in the back of your legs and the small of your back spring to life to help hold you up and move you around. Now consider that recess in your sole called the arch. If you spend a good deal of time on your feet, unsupported arches can sag and may fall out of shape altogether. (This is why in those pre-cruiser days a policeman was known as a flatfoot.) To help prevent your arches from falling, Roots are contoured to support them. There's a smaller recess between the balls of your feet which Roots will take care of as well.

Near the front, you'll notice the sole is curved like a rocker. In normal walking, your weight lands first on your heel, shifts along the outer side of your foot, then diagonally across to your big toe which springs you off on your next step. The rocker idea simply makes that transfer of weight a little easier, which makes each step a little less tiring.

All told, Roots bring a good, natural feeling to man's somewhat un-natural custom of treading hard floors and city sidewalks. Roots are designed and made in Canada; and at the heart of our production are two generations of cobblers (a father and three sons) who cling to the premise that good quality footwear must still be made largely by hand. The way we feel about making Roots has a lot to do with the way you'll feel wearing them.

roots
NATURAL FOOTWEAR

City feet need Roots.

fig 8.10

girls! do it every afternoon!

Watch the great daytime programming on CBC Television. Information, laughter, excitement, love with:

TAKE THIRTY

LUNCHEON DATE

55 NORTH MAPLE

THE EDGE OF NIGHT

THE GALLOPING GOURMET

CBC ...a great way to spend the afternoon

fig 8.11

P. Wkly Nov 10

On the pill...or pregnant. Two reasons to learn the pure facts about orange juice.

ads 1975

When it comes to nutritional needs, women on the pill and women who are pregnant have something in common. They both have an increased need for a very important vitamin known as folic acid.

What does folic acid do?
Folic acid plays a necessary role in the making of new cells. Since this also pertains to the making of red blood cells, without sufficient folic acid, you could become anemic. If you're on the pill or pregnant, ask your doctor to tell you more. Help insure against a folic acid deficiency by knowing

which foods contain high amounts of this essential vitamin. Examples are green, leafy vegetables, liver, and 100% pure orange juice.

Why is orange juice such a good source of folic acid?
Not only does orange juice supply a plentiful amount of folic acid, you drink it in its pure, natural state. That's important because in cooking, you can destroy up to 95% of the folic acid in foods.
Those are the pure facts. Isn't it nice to know that something so delicious can be so good for you?

© State of Florida, Department of Citrus, 1975

100% PURE ORANGE JUICE FROM FLORIDA

fig 8.12

36

New Clover Leaf Chunk Light Tuna – rich and satisfying – is for tuna-loving budget watchers. Get several tins next time you're shopping.

Product of British Columbia Packers Limited who also bring you Rupert Brand Fresh Frozen Seafoods

fig 8.13

Introducing new quilted Pampers. They stay twice as dry as cloth.

Tests show that new quilted Pampers stay twice as dry as cloth diapers. The soft quilted lining helps keep the wetness down in the padding, away from your baby's skin. Now your baby can be more comfortable. In new quilted Pampers. When a baby's more comfortable, he's much happier.

New quilted Pampers stay nice 'n dry. Twice as dry as cloth.

fig 8.15

Don't waste Habitant Soups on times like these, please.

. . . unless you want to make ordinary days special. Habitant Soup <u>is</u> special — slowly, patiently simmered to give you full, undiluted flavour — the home-made flavour you <u>never add water to</u>.

P.S. There are 10 different delectable flavours: Pea, Vegetable, Chicken Noodle, Chicken Rice, Tomato Vermicelli, Beef Consommé with Sherry, Onion, Cabbage, and two new additions — Pea Soup with Ham, and Minestrone.

Habitant Soups. Something out of the ordinary.

fig 8.14

Welch's. THE GRAPE FACTORY.

A wonderful place, the Grape Factory. We have fun with grapes. We turn them into drinks, concentrates, jams and jellies – as naturally as we can, so that you may enjoy the true flavour of our Great Canadian Grapes.

For healthy, happy families everywhere in Canada.

Welch's. Closer to nature.

fig 8.16

MAPLE LEAF BACON

fig 8.17

1980 - 1989

1980
Pierre Trudeau
re-elected Prime Minister

1980
Terry Fox runs
Marathon of Hope

Following a period of social upheaval demanded by a generation committed to creating change, the 1980s became seen as a decade of excess and decadence. Post baby-boomers were dubbed "generation X" by author Douglas Coupland and described as self-centred and disillusioned with society.

On May 20, 1980, referendum day in Quebec, the emotional reaction of separatists who lost to the federalist campaign would demonstrate the division that threatened Canada. The demographics of the country rapidly changed. A population explosion among First Nations peoples contributed to a more confident and stronger native community, vocal in their fight for justice and land. Whereas prior to 1961, over 80% of immigrants were from Europe, from 1981-1990, approximately 50% of immigrants were of Asian and/or Middle Eastern origin. However, while Canadian society was visibly becoming more multicultural and diverse, this was not reflected in advertising images.

Women began to gain recognition in this decade. In 1982, Bertha Wilson became the first woman appointed to the Supreme Court. Two years later, Jeanne Sauve was appointed Governor General, another first for women. Other women broke into the boardrooms of large corporations: Betty Kennedy of the Bank of Montreal, and Gail Clark of Manufacturers Life are two important examples. The buying power of women grew even though women were still significantly disadvantaged by the gender wage gap.

Canadian culture was also maturing. Film, music, and writing gained international recognition. In 1982, Trudeau fulfilled his commitment to constitutional reform with the repatriation of the Constitution. Without a consensus among all provinces, however, constitutional issues were far from resolved. The failure of the Meech Lake Accord revealed a Canada with a divided vision of its future, as various groups sought more control over their interests.

CANADIAN LAUNCHES A $2.4 BILLION SPACE PROGRAM.

This summer, four new space craft will be flying daily between Vancouver, Toronto, Calgary and Montreal.

Twenty more wide-body 767-300 Extended Range jetliners are planned.

At a cost of $2.4 billion. A measure of just how committed we are to providing you with the best schedule, the best fleet, the best service in the air.

The flight management system is the most modern in the sky.

The spacious interior of the 767-300 ER is designed to give you a superior level of comfort.

This new generation of aircraft also heralds the return of our world-renowned *First Class* service on major transcon routes.

In *Canadian Class* our

The comforts of Canadian Class.

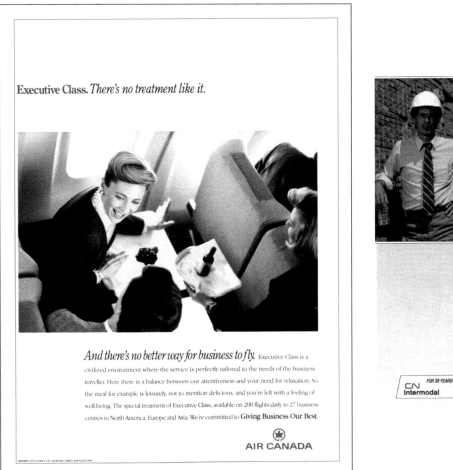

Executive Class. *There's no treatment like it.*

And there's no better way for business to fly. Executive Class is a civilized environment where the service is perfectly tailored to the needs of the business traveller. Here there is a balance between our attentiveness and your need for relaxation. So the meal for example is leisurely, not to mention delicious, and you're left with a feeling of well-being. The special treatment of Executive Class, available on 200 flights daily to 27 business centres in North America, Europe and Asia. We're committed to **Giving Business Our Best.**

AIR CANADA

CN Intermodal   FOR 35 YEARS!

fig 9.2

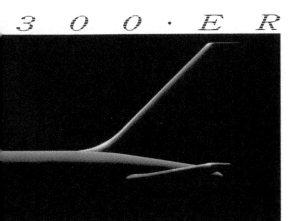

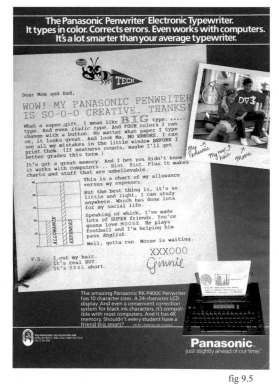

fig 9.6

fig 9.7

fig 9.8

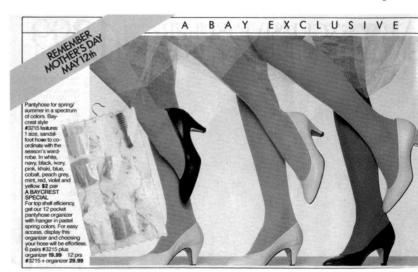

fig 9.9

1990 - 1999

1990
Creation of the World
Wide Web/Internet

1991
Goods and services tax
(GST) is introduced

The 1990s solidified the rise of youth, with Generation Y being recognized as a key contributor to Canadian society. More self-assured and confident than its predecessor, Generation Y became the new target of advertisers. Magazines and stores began catering to tweens and teens. Advertisers scrambled to understand what appealed to this new sophisticated group of adolescents through marketing surveys and analyses. Ads continued to target Generation X, especially with products for their offspring.

In the cities, Canada's diverse population became the norm. In 1999, Adrienne Clarkson, a refugee whose family fled China in 1942, was named Governor General of Canada. Increasingly, women were recognized as a key consumer group and advertisers for products such as cars began to target females. Gender and diversity portrayal guidelines were established by Advertising Standards Canada in 1994, in an effort to promote equity in the media.

The North American Free Trade Agreement (NAFTA) signed in 1993 brought closer economic ties with the United States. Outside of the provisions of free trade, the music industry and "Hollywood North" boomed. More than anything else, the information age transformed Canadian industry and economics. Kanata, a suburb of Ottawa, became known as Silicon Valley North. More and more Canadian workers found jobs in electronics while jobs in heavy manufacturing industries shrank. Along with radio and television, the Internet became an integral part of Canadian households. Advertising was transformed by e-commerce. The Internet Advertising Bureau was formed to provide Internet publishers, advertisers, and agencies a collective voice in the support and development of interactive advertising.

Despite conflict and change throughout the 1990s, Canada entered the 21st century as a growing and prosperous nation.

fig 10.1

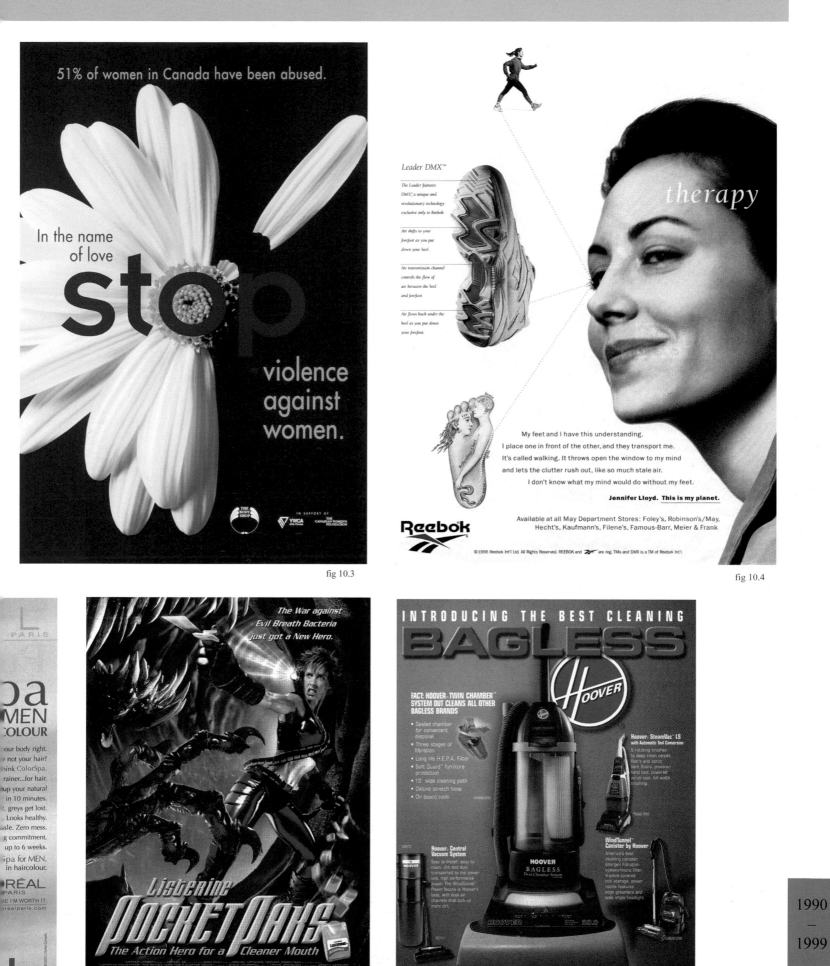

fig 10.3

fig 10.4

fig 10.2

fig 10.5

fig 10.6

1990
—
1999

43

1995	1997	1997	1998
Internet trading company ebay founded	Jean Chretien re-elected Prime Minister	Internet Advertising Bureau established	*Titanic*, directed by Canadian filmmaker James Cameron

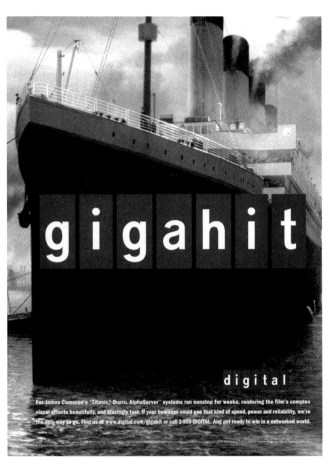

gigahit

digital

For James Cameron's "Titanic," Digital AlphaServer™ systems ran nonstop for weeks, rendering the film's complex visual effects beautifully, and blazingly fast. If your business could use that kind of speed, power and reliability, we're the only way to go. Find us at www.digital.com/gigahit or call 1-800-DIGITAL. And get ready to win in a networked world.

fig 10.7

Black tie optional.

Think different.™

fig 10.8

Everybody doing business directly— *To me that's the power of the Internet.*

New Dell PowerEdge™ Servers

My name is Michael Dell. I like to think of myself as an innovator who started a company, Dell Computer, around an idea: that everybody should be doing business directly with one another—one-to-one, with no barriers.

Today, the Internet is making that even more true, by enabling us all to establish direct relationships with our customers.

That's certainly true here. Once we start a relationship with you, we'll help you determine how best to integrate the Internet into your business.

At Dell, being direct is a philosophy of creating value for our customers. And it's our reason for being.

1-800-296-7160

Visit www.dell.com/innovator to learn more about how our new enterprise products, software, technology consulting and team of professionals can help make the Internet work for your business.

intel inside
Pentium III xeon

Dell offers a complete line of Intel-based systems. Simplify your e-business with robust Dell PowerEdge servers based on the Pentium III Xeon™ processor, including the Dell PowerEdge™ 8450 Server. This monster can accommodate up to eight Pentium III Xeon processors, up to ten 64-bit PCI slots and is expandable to 32GB RAM.

BE DIRECT™
D∈LL
www.dell.ca

fig 10.9

This has your name on it.

VISA GOLD

Luckily, so does this.

All you need.™

fig 10.10

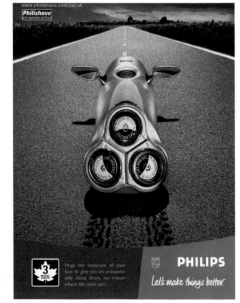

www.philishave.com/norisk
Philishave WITH QUADRA ACTION

3

Hugs the contours of your face to give you an unexpectedly close shave, no matter where life takes you.

PHILIPS
Let's make things better

fig 10.11

44

The Halifax Chronicle Herald, June 2, 1995

Programmer – We are seeking a qualified programmer to provide support to our administrative systems development team-applicants should possess post secondary education in computer science and must have experience in COBOL and RDB UNDER VMS. Knowledge of the DIGITAL ALPHA PLATFORM and General Accounting Principles will be considered assets.

Subway – Position available for mature individual-must be available for the close shift (until 4 a.m.) Clean appearance, friendly, good math and problem solving skills.

fig 10.12

fig 10.13

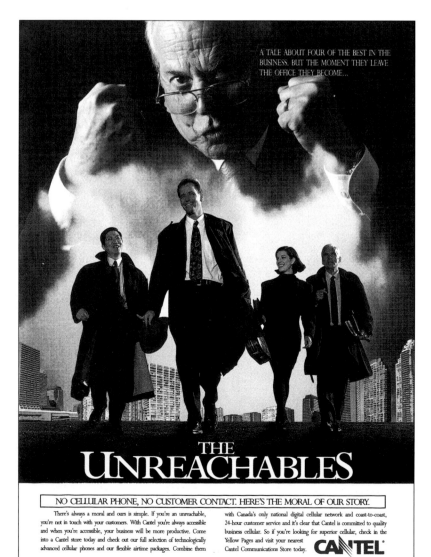

fig 10.14

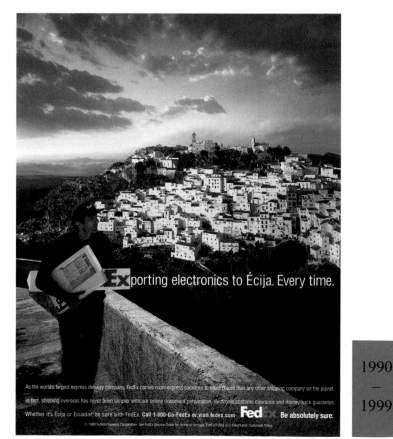

fig 10.15

45

Into the 21st Century

Elspeth Lynn and Lorraine Tao, award-winning creative partners, formed Zig, a Toronto-based agency in 1999.

"For decades, women have been spoken to through the voice of men. This is simply because historically, creative departments of advertising agencies have been populated mainly by men. While there has been significant change in the last ten years, women still represent the minority. So naturally, through no real fault of their own, male creatives have tended to create advertising for women from a distinctly male perspective.

In the past, advertising has prescribed how women should look, act and feel. We believe the new way to reach women is to leave those things open for interpretation and speak to women through insight and emotion. Too often we try to speak to 'mothers,' 'house-wives' or 'women juggling a career and kids.' We believe the way to speak to the masses isn't through stereotypes. It's through insights that all women can relate to."

DON'T LET IT MEASURE YOUR SELF-ESTEEM.

Kellogg's Special K

Look good on your own terms.

fig 11.1

Jenna finally got invited to a school friend's birthday party.

Imagine how she feels.

EDUCATION

Help make a difference.

INCLUSION

That's what we do.

UNDERSTANDING

ASSOCIATION FOR COMMUNITY LIVING

Helping people with an intellectual disability.

fig 11.2

Explore five hundred channels. You'll never find one with fresh air. It's what we were thinking when we redesigned the all new 2002 Explorer. Now smoother, roomier and more powerful. Discover why nothing is better at taking you away and bringing you together all at the same time. There's an Explorer in all of us.

THE ALL NEW 2002 EXPLORER
- OPTIONAL 3RD ROW SEAT – seats seven • AVAILABLE ALL ALUMINUM V8 – more power
- ADVANCED REAR LIFT GATE – easy loading • ADVANCED SAFETY FEATURES – peace of mind
- ROOMIER INTERIOR – added comfort • INDEPENDENT REAR SUSPENSION – smoother ride

Ford

NO BOUNDARIES

www.ford.ca

fig 11.3

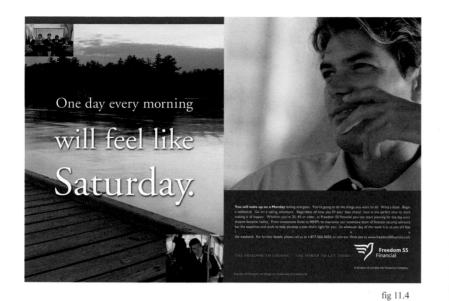

One day every morning

will feel like

Saturday.

fig 11.4

Imagine if the only person you

had to answer to

was you.

Freedom
Financial

THE FREEDOM TO CHOOSE. THE POWER TO GET THERE.

fig 11.5

fig 11.6

Fact sheet on the advertising industry (2001)

- Total world advertising expenditure in measured media projected for 2001 is $481.1 billion, an increase of 3.7% over 2000
- Direct and indirect employment in this sector represented approximately 250 000 jobs, or about 2% of all jobs in Canada.
- Approximately 79% of total advertising expenditures in Canada remain in the Canadian economy.
- Approximately $2.5 billion is invested in Canada annually in television advertising and about $1 billion in radio advertising.
- Advertising is the single largest contributor of funds to the Canadian television broadcasting system.

Gender Portrayal Guidelines (1994)

The Gender Portrayal Guidelines contain 6 clauses. Key commitments include:
- The equal portrayal of men and women as single decision-makers regarding purchases; and the portrayal of women and men as equal participants in joint decision-making in the workplace and at home
- Avoiding the inappropriate use or exploitation of sexuality.

Examples provided by the guidelines include the following:

-people must not be portrayed as primarily sexual or defined by their sexuality

-boys and girls under 16 must not be portrayed as displaying adult sexual characteristics

-using or displaying a woman's sexuality in order to sell a product that has no relation to sexuality is by definition sexually exploitative

-sexual harassment must not be portrayed as normal behaviour and women should not be represented as objects of uncontrolled desire

- No violence or domination of one sex over the other, either with overt or implied threats, or actual force
- The portrayal of women and men in fully diverse roles and as equally competent in a wide range of activities, both inside and outside the home
- Avoiding language that misrepresents, offends or excludes women or men

- Advertising Standards Canada

Acknowledgments

The Publishers gratefully acknowledge the many corporations who kindly granted us permission to reproduce their advertisements in this book. We are especially grateful for the help and support we received from the Hudson's Bay Company's Heritage Services Department and ZIG.

Absorbine - registered trademark of W.F. Young Incorporated

Air Canada

Apple Computer Incorporated

Association for Community Living – Courtesy of ForbesDesignGroupIncorporated

Austin Automobiles

Avon Products Incorporated

Bell Canada

Bendix Aviation – registered trademark of Honeywell International Incorporated

Bethlehem Steel Corporation

BFGoodrich Tire Company

British Columbia Packers

Canada Dry Ginger Ale – registered trademark of Dr. Pepper / Seven Up Incorporated

Canada Packers Limited

Canada Post

Canadian Airlines

Canadian Army – Department of National Defense

Canadian Broadcasting Corporation

Canadian Imperial Bank of Commerce

Canadian National Railway Company

Canadian Pacific Railway Company Archives

Canadian Tire Corporation Limited

Canon Incorporated

Cantel - registered trademark of Rogers AT & T Wireless

CCM - registered trademark of Pro Cycle Group

Charles Atlas

Chevrolet – a registered trademark of General Motors of Canada Limited

Chic Zippers – registered trademark of Coats the Threadmakers

Clover Leaf Seafoods

Coleman Corporation

Coppertone - registered trademark of Schering-Plough Health Care Products

Coty Incorporated

Dell Computer Corporation

Digital Equipment of Canada

Dodge – registered trademark of Daimler Chrysler Corporation

Eaton's – a division of Sears Canada Incorporated

Estate of Charlie Chaplin

FedEx Corporation

Florida Department of Citrus

ForbesDesignGroupIncorporated

Ford Motor Company of Canada Limited

General Electric Company of Canada

Gregg College - copyright of McGraw-Hill Publishing

Habitant Soup - registered trademark of Campbell Soup Company

Havoline - registered trademark of Chevron Texaco Corporation

Hoover Company – a division of Maytag

Hudson's Bay Company – Heritage Services Department

Ivory - registered trademark of Proctor & Gamble

Special K – registered trademark of Kellogg Company

Kleenex – registered trademark of Kimberly-Clarke

Kodak – Eastman Kodak Company

L'Oreal Group International

LA Gear – registered trademark of ACI

Lake Simcoe Ice & Fuel Company

Levi Strauss Company

Life Humor Magazine

Listerine - registered trademark of Pfizer Canada Inc. / Warner Lambert Consumer Group

Lockheed / Trans Canada - registered trademarks of Air Canada

London Life Insurance Company

Manufacturer's Life - registered trademark of Manulife Financial

Maple Leaf Foods International

McLaughlin Carriage Company - registered trademark of General Motors of Canada

National Liberal Committee

Neilson's - registered trademark of Cadbury Trebor Allan

Nestle Canada Incorporated

Nupron - registered trademark of Honeywell International Inc.

One-a-Day – copyright Bayer Corporation

Palmolive – registered trademark of Colgate-Palmolive Company

Pampers - registered trademark of Procter & Gamble

Pears Soap - registered trademark of Unilever

Pepsi / Pepsi-Cola - registered trademarks of Pepsico Inc.

Philips - registered trademark of Koninklijke Philips Electronics

Pontiac - registered trademark of General Motors of Canada

Quasar / Panasonic – registered trademarks of Panasonic Canada Incorporated

RC Cola – Royal Crown Company Incorporated

RCA Victor Group

Reebok International Limited

Renfrew Electric Company Limited

Rogers Communications Incorporated

Roots Canada Limited

Royal Bank of Canada

Russell Automobile - registered trademark of Canada Cycle & Motor Company

Sal Hepatica - registered trademark of Bristol-Myers Pharmaceutical Institute

Scott Tissue – registered trademark of Kimberly-Clark

Sunlight Soap - registered trademark of Unilever

The Body Shop – courtesy of ForbesDesignGroupIncorporated

The Boeing Company

The Gillette Company

The Globe and Mail

The Halifax Chronicle Herald

The Swatch Group

The Toronto Daily Star

Tilden - registered trademark of ANC

Travel Alberta Tourism

Tyco Toys – registered trademark of Mattel Incorporated

Vaseline - registered trademark of Unilever

VISA International

Volkswagen of Canada

Waterman Pen Company

Welchs – National Grape Cooperative Association Incorporated

Westinghouse Electric Company LLC – BNFL Group Company

Workopolis – a division of Bell Globe Media & The Toronto Star

YMCA Canada